# we are a galaxy

Also by Sephyrus Press

Sappho Does Hay(na)ku, by Scott Keeney

No Fresh Cut Flowers: An Afterlife Anthology, edited by Rachel Archelaus

Intuitive Art: How to Have a Two-Way Conversation with Your Higher Self, by Rachel Archelaus

Above the Surface, by Rachel Archelaus & Scott Keeney

I Am Powerful, by Amy F. Pilato

# we are a galaxy

Poems, prose, & illustrations by,
Rachel Archelaus

SEPHYRUS PRESS

*"If I truly love one person, I love all people, I love the world, I love life."*

Eric Fromm

# Table of Contents

Love can be lusty, cosmic, and confusing.
It's always multidimensional.

we are a galaxy

# Waking up Tired

Whenever I wake up this tired, I know I've been places. Hard at work in dreamland means two things: meeting up with people I am working with and letting go of deep issues. Two nights ago, I had the best possible dream. We were in a grassy area next to a stream. The grass was so vibrant green it had a blue aura, how I imagine Tennessee to be. We were shy with each other at first. You barely looked at me, but when you did, it was with the same telling eyes as always. I knew what you wanted to know, and it didn't take me long to spill it. "You know I'm in love with you, right?" You melted a little at this. You were happy to hear that it's real. I was happy to see you standing your ground, not running away like I always imagined you would. "I want to get to know you better," I followed. Ease. We can be friends.

# First Kiss 1: Living Room

Paneling on the wall, Bradlees nightgown, a three and a half foot tall little girl. Long white-blonde hair and the biggest smile around, even when brownie batter wasn't covering her face. Talking to grown-ups was much more fun for her than making friends her own age. She's so social that she doesn't need preschool, according to her mother. This is the 80s, and long before Baby Einstein. Mud pies and climbing trees in the front yard are better than organized recess. She only watched television on Saturday mornings, and Taxi was her favorite show. Andy Kaufman was her clown. She woke up extra early on Saturdays and slipped into her Minnie Mouse leotard just in time for Mousercise. Even though she could do many things by herself, she still needed to wake her parents up, oh so gently, so they could turn on the TV.

This girl was at home in the world. She superimposed her imagination on everything, so the house, the restaurants her family frequented, and her beloved backyard all felt custom-made. She learned how to plant seeds from her neighbor and how to be patient enough to harvest pinky-sized carrots in a few weeks. The tiny sprouts of hair they grew were the marker that the sweet orange sticks were growing below. She tried to catch leprechauns in the front yard with her version of a snare trap. She knew their path through the yard, so catching one was inevitable. Her best friends of all were the praying mantises that congregated on the back fence and shed. Their sticky feet clung to the rough wood covered in light gray paint. The contrast of their green bodies helped her find them each morning. She could talk to them for hours while she swung next to them on the play set. Each had a name which changed every day.

One day, she and her mom were in the living room saying goodbye to Dad as he left for work. Mom gave him a hug and a kiss. As our girl looked up between the towering adults, she wiggled in her position on his feet, hugging his legs so he wouldn't go. He enjoyed the game they enacted every day. "Don't go! Let's play!" But every day, he'd bend down, his face getting closer to hers to kiss her before exiting. This day, she lifted her head to meet his and planted her tiny lips on his. His mustache felt like a toothbrush held against her cupid's bow. Before they parted contact, she pushed her tongue past her teeth, through the crack in her mouth until it was met with a sudden backwards jerk.

No sound was uttered, just a look of shock. An "OH!" shape on his face. Mom didn't understand, and then Dad said, "We don't kiss family members like that." The girl was embarrassed and unsure what she had done wrong. Her face now distorted and unsure of how to be, where to hide herself. Mom came over and gave her a hug from behind, cradling her with her long arms. "It's ok, sweetie." The two adults were now chuckling, and this seemed to ease the tension. Dad turned around and left for the day after making sure his daughter had recovered.

In the same room, six years later, the girl had a birthday party. She wanted to play cool games and hang out with the cool kids, so she decided not to invite her best friend, Cherry. This set in motion a series of events that would unfold over the years and involve Cherry's sister Jess. One time on the bus, Jess said she didn't like it that the girl wore two different colored socks. Cherry didn't invite the girl to her next birthday party as revenge, and she even got a pony to come so the girl would feel extra bad. No one was aware that these things would happen, though.

The cool kids were over, and everyone was seated around the coffee table. A few kids were on the couch, and some were on the floor with the girl. They started playing Truth or Dare. The cutest boy at the party was sitting on the couch. He was hunched over himself so he could hear the others talking. He had short brown hair and a small nose. The most alluring thing about him was his quiet, feminine nature. He was a cool guy and a skater, but he was thin-boned and wafty. The girl invited him because she wanted to kiss him. She wanted her thin lips to touch his thin face, anywhere.

The first dares and truths were a blur. She was so nervous that she couldn't keep up with what was happening. Heart pounding, eyes darting, Crystal (the coolest girl), looking aloof in the elbow of the couch, was sitting next to the girl's crush. Would Crystal get to kiss him? Wait, it's Crystal's turn to dare the girl! Since Crystal didn't really know the girl that well, she didn't know to dare her to kiss cool guy. When the directive started flowing from Crystal's mouth, she listened so closely so that she wouldn't forget. Each word playing over and over in the girl's mind so it would stick, "Go, go, go, go and lick, lick, lick, cool guy's, cool guy's, cool guy's, big, big, big, big, big, big, toe, toe, toe, toe, toe, toe, toe, toe. Wait, what?! Lick his toe!?!????"

The tremors started as she inched her way over to the couch like a caterpillar. He took off his sock, placed it neatly next to his thigh. It would be smelly and sweaty, she thought. He extended his shin and pointed that big toe right at her. She couldn't waste time butt scooting over to him any longer. She was there. The toe was out, ready to be licked. Her face lowered and craned over to his foot. She pushed her tongue slowly out of its parking spot and held her breath. She didn't want the stink of his foot to throw her off. She had to do this in one try. The form she chose was simple. No upward licking movement, no, this was not ice cream. She wanted a quick touch of the tip of her tongue to be enough. It would leave a wet mark and probably cause him to scream. That would do. Now her tongue, almost there, closing in, "AHH!" Everyone yelped when contact was made.

More dares were made, more truths were revealed. She wasn't paying attention. She was still fixated on a kiss.

Finally, her turn came again, and she proudly declared that she wanted another dare. She was brave and hoped that her new cool-kid friends would not try to top their last dare with something even grosser. Luckily, it wasn't Crystal telling the girl what to do; it was a guy. As the girl waited for her orders, she felt pretty OK. She had her hands behind her, leaning back into them. She looked like she was on a pool lounger, but with her legs crossed. She felt accomplished and like she'd proven that she could take the hard challenges and meet them with her eyes open.

Once she heard the dare, she started to feel a little cocky. She had to because she had lied immediately upon hearing it. The dare was to French kiss Joey, the mildly cute neighbor. They asked her if she'd done it before, and she, of course, said yes. Everyone had the perception that she was sexually advanced, not that she'd had sex, but that she at least knew how to French kiss. This may have been because she was always the first to ask a boy to dance and because she called up Adam on the phone in second grade to ask him out. The truth was that she loved boys and that she was very well liked by them, but she felt like an outsider. She wasn't sure why people liked her. She would assume that no one would invite her to their parties and that her track coach wouldn't call her by name to lead the warm-up laps. This lack of social understanding sometimes appeared as fearlessness.

When Joey came over to her spot on the floor, the girl moved from sitting cross-legged to perching on her knees. She perked up, almost looking like an angel with her blonde hair and straight back. He came into her space and she closed her eyes. Waiting for the touch of his smooth lips to hers, she inhaled and exhaled through her nose. She didn't reach out her hands or think about anything too deeply. At the first lip-to-lip sensation, she actually relaxed. It was exhilarating! It made her feel alive and like a rope that had been coiled within her torso was now being wildly tossed about. And then she felt wet. His tongue peeked through the crack in his mouth and was hitting up against her puckered lips. She recoiled so suddenly that her hands caught her, and again she looked like she was reclining near the pool. Joey was confused; they all were. "I thought you'd done that before?" Joey asked. "I have!" she said, searching her brain for a good excuse to tell. Nothing came. She decided to wipe the moment from her memory and not let it get in the way of enjoying the sight of the beautiful, wafty boy who was still sitting on her couch.

# To a Man

Your
marshmallow cocoon
is quite intoxicating

# Cosmo Night

Because I laugh.
Because you
do,

too. I can't
say no
more.

Sea gulls? Herons?
God? ha
ha.

There isn't an
answer to
this.

I am not
untouchable. I'm
not

anything which has
a name.
Why

is this form
useful? How
did

it become so?
You. You
are

the connection to
this burp

of

cosmo. Ask me
not why.
I

wish I knew.
Galaxy creation.
Stars

as child. "You
will have
a

boy and girl,"
she said.
"You

will meet your
love at
higher

elevation."
Foretelling? I
do not know!

I take it
as it
comes.

You are here.
No others
near.

It goes reaching
for what
I...

know or not.
It moves
me.

Trecero

Where does my smoke go when
I exhale, and why do you always
know what will make me smile?
Always caught between myself.
Which should I be right now?
Eyes change dark to fluorescent
every day. Every day, every day.
You know there is no influencer
now? I threw it in the trash.
Folded in two. Like midnight,
they came and went. Illuminated
and space. Onto your cigarettes.
Lost at darkness, not. Better
able to see with the eyes open.
You're floating, peeping in, I like.
Would love to see you more. You
looked small today, shocked. I
could kiss you. Would kiss you.
Want to. None better time than
in spirit. But not again, this
mix of real. Which one is it?
Romanced by something I can't
understand. Now that interference
is immaterial. Shouting, louder.
Me, on me, myself, who now?
Getting there. Paint a picture.

# Burning

It burns here.
Under the
river.

That sand is
yellow and
red.

It's telling me
to be
silent.

Hold your breath
and listen.
______.

And

Happy man or
old dying
man

# One Minute

I am not writing as myself
because I am at someone
else's keyboard. I just noticed
how one minute apart means that
time is not made of jelly.
One minute apart means that
time, being a slick friend
who calls you a nickname
you hate, is just there, waiting
for you at every turn to tell
you how wrong you are to feel
the way you do and how wrong
you are to keep feeling those
feelings. Time just sits
and waits for you to notice him
clicking, ticking away until
you give in, and as Bukoswki once
said, throw the radio out the
window. You want to look at the
cute lady across the way, whose
ass is shining at you while she
gardens but... Time will get
you. He'll steal your courage
and send you into something.
That something you don't want
to say.

## Adrenaline

He sits her on a wooden bench scented with plausibility.
Circling dove mourning cries, gray and white, winged,
a pair landing.
Parachute touch down.
Weathered hand still feminine calls his face to palm.
The hand cups his uneven texture.
Soft fleece jacket over his abdomen, syncopated heartbeat
visible.
A flicker of brown iris in the still moment of union
served to her; he is gracious.
Now the lips part, curling.
Heat hit the ears and color the cheeks raised in smile.
Palm to thigh of singular.
Relapse to her last chance adrenaline rising hard.
She states it. Thick distraction-laden window
pausing leaf falling mid-air disco ball to pierce
eyelids open, hearts, mouths to connect.
To keep spinning.

Crush

Driving by the overfilled stream on the way to work, I saw you. You were wearing the orange-and-blue striped shirt that was two sizes too big. Your faded black jeans were wet up to the knees. If we were kids, I would have pushed you in the water. You'd get soaked, and then you could blame it all on me. Your mom would ask me not to do that ever again because you catch colds so easily. I would say, "Yes, of course, I'm really sorry." Then we would walk outside and sit on the driveway so you could dry off in the sun.

I'd lie back and get little bits of gravel in my hair, and we'd close our eyes to see what shapes appear behind our eyelids. We'd be good friends. Easy. It doesn't work that way anymore, though. I didn't stop the car; I kept driving by. I'm home now. The image is still in my mind. I should have stopped and pushed you. Maybe I've just lost my nerve.

What if I had pulled over and gotten out of the car? Maybe you would look away after seeing me and pretend that I wasn't coming up behind you. The noise of my sneakers crunching leaves and branches brushing my jeans would keep your face locked on the water. When I was close enough, I would touch your sleeve with my hand, making sure to only disrupt the fabric. I've never touched you before.

For my benefit, I reserve your reactions to be plain and dry. I would accept anything from you. I've always known that I am one word away from being told to fuck off. Your reaction is not for me; it is for you. So you can feel whole, not alone. You had to try. But after you turn around and show me your face, down on the bank of the stream, I would push you in.
I believe this act is larger than I ever imagined. Whatever brought my eyes down to the stream today is more than I

can fight off. Whatever brought your feet into that stream is telling me that you are with me. That's all I need to know.

Ta-ta for now.

To speak- length.
Not taken,
not

undone.
Intersect, maybe
not. Intercede it,

yes.  Post it.
Please laugh.
Please

ease.
This vacuum.
Hurts with chill.

Heats with something.
In time.
Bye.

# Meditation

Your energy is like a blanket heaved at me with no regard for timespace. It Caspers my head, and even though I can see through the loose weave, everything is effervescent and golden. There's no way to take off the blanket unless I trick myself into believing that it was there all along. In which case, the gold is part of me, and there's nothing to feel awkward about. It's silly how many fables your face appears in and how many meditative moments are absorbed by your beating heart in my hands. I'm too old for games now, maybe poetry too, but too scared to be direct. Still worried about sanctity and shit like that. Upsetting the unit and all. As I sit on my not-sky-blue cushion, I clear my mind of passing prose and future lines. Yet the golden fizz still exists. Maybe the blanket image isn't working anymore because it's not a filter. This telepathy or dimensional bond could be (ha) something real. With those fuzzy threads reaching out to be unraveled. Maybe it's my job to share from my open wound of a soul. About how you helped me realize that love goes far beyond physical manifestation. And that even though my original vision for what human coming together could be failed miserably, you were there to help me through it. And here you are now, just when I've redefined what it means to be a person on this planet with more delight to share than she knows what to do with. So why you keep showing up in my meditations appears simple. You've been there for my heart awakenings and wall breakings, and now it's my turn to be there for you.

Long sentences

Maybe I was kind of done
but then I had a dream
that entailed a minivan
and a driver who was
spinning us around town
in a circle, and then my wife
was gone somewhere, shopping
or something, and we were in
the back seat.

Nothing happened
really, except that we
didn't speak to each other-
which is plausible if it were
real life, but the flick of an
index finger upon your
curled up hand sitting
next to your thigh.

That's all it took.

So then the dream ended
and before I could transpose
the people as I am doing now,
I inlaid many other
scenarios that I wish had
happened.

Oh Shit

We're the same thing.
I never even thought of that.
too scared to draw the eyes.

## Welcomed Frustration

so actually...how
do we
put

up with this?
basic human
wanting

has been disabled
after all...
shame.

see,
there is
room for more.

(Must be read with a Cowboy accent)

Picked up this page turner at work a few years ago.
Have you read it? It's all about these two dreamers
who can't catch hold of each other. Hard as they try,
they've never so much as grazed the other's shoulder.
As a neutral party, I can tell you it's a shame. A growing
dynamo waiting to erupt. Been too long now to clear
the air. They may as well pretend there's no mountain
gas between 'em.

Space

In the end, there was space, and there was mountain.

Rebecca?

My name is Rachel, but yes?

We live on an island in outer space. It's called, never mind. Our air is neon yellow, orange, and slate. Are you OK with that?

Yes.

Would you prefer a water residence or one with a view?

Both, please.

Very well. Which patch would you like to call home? You can slide down any color at any time.

I like the tallest, please. Red.

We only have tan available. That was a trick question.

This is a little frustrating. Can't you just take me there?

Of course.

　　Update:

I witnessed my first inverse sunset tonight. From the top of Tan Mountain, where I can slide down into the ocean.

I have changed my name to Rebecca. But also go by Stan.

My children are to remain at home, on Earth.

I have brought my cat Bucky (Purr Buckminster the Pony).

He is pleased with this location. And with the gorny weevils to chase.

Galaxy

When you look up
in your backyard

past the tallest leaves,
that's us.

We made that.
I don't have proof yet.

That doesn't really
interest me.

But I have to know,
Do you see it, too?

# First Kiss 2: Sledding

Jordan showed up unexpectedly from Southbury. He was very tall for a sixth grader and spiked up his blue hair to add a few more inches. He wore CK-1 instead of deodorant and was raised by his mother. Jordan was a mystery in a sea of the familiar. The girl had known most of her classmates since kindergarten. She felt like it was a game to learn about him. He used to pass her notes in science class, which she collected and put in tiny metal tins to preserve their scent.

Jordan asked her out almost immediately after arriving in town. She thought it was because of the purple streaks in her hair. They were a visual match, except that when he hugged her, his arms wrapped around her head rather than her waist. Having a real boyfriend was new. Sure, she'd held hands at dances, hung out with guys in the park, she even had a friend who climbed in her window when her parents were running errands, but no one had ever been dedicated to her like this. When she called his house, his tired mother would put her hand over the receiver and shout, "Jorrrrrdaaaaaan, it's your girllllllfrieeeeeeeend." This always made the girl blush.

Dave, the friend with window privileges, was friends with Jordan and quickly became the couple's translator. Dave would show up and assert Jordan's needs. The girl would then negotiate a settlement and send Dave back home. One day, Dave showed up in Jen's living room to deliver a message. The girl could tell that Dave was nervous about this one. He was sweaty and had a half smile on his face. Dave wasn't a particularly finessed human being, so they could all tell that something big was about to come out of his mouth. The girls stopped him from walking in circles and put their arms on his lumpy shoulders. "What is it?" Jen asked.

Dave sighed reluctantly and, before speaking, took on a more confident posture. He then blurted out Jordan's no-longer-secret desire: he wanted to go all the way.

This really threw our girl off. She paced, laughed, and showed her teeth. Jen was more experienced than the girl, and even she was concerned. A blow job, maybe, but not real sex. The girl wasn't ready! They started to wonder about Southbury. Was this normal behavior? The girl collected herself and stood squarely in front of Dave. She asked him what he thought. Would Jordan break up with her if she didn't go through with this? He wasn't sure, but he did suggest she do it.

The girl stood there for a moment with her head down. Once she was ready, she thoughtfully spoke her answer to the room. She would not go all the way; that was too much. He hadn't even kissed her yet! And if he wanted to break up with her, he could. The girls dispatched Dave off to Jordan's house and regrouped to discuss the scandalous request in more detail.

Jen, Dave, Jordan, and the girl all had science class together. The boys sat at the middle table, and the girls sat in the back with Heather. Each group discussed their sides of the situation. Sideways glances, chewed gum, and tiny balls of paper were flung about for 45 minutes. Mr. Sayers, had checked out of teaching long ago. He didn't even check the homework sheets. Once the kids realized this, they began inserting foul scenarios where they should have been explaining mitosis and other miracles of life. Eventually, the teacher caught on and had a few words with the girl's parents. He told them she was boy-crazy.

It was winter in Connecticut, and new snow had just fallen. The protocol for this situation was to bring your plastic sled up to the path behind the High School. It was a long walk, but worth it once you got there. Jordan, Dave, the girl, and some others went first thing Saturday morning. Jordan's coat looked old, and his green striped knit hat resembled something a grandma would make. The girl realized that Jordan wasn't from a comfortable financial situation like she was. She understood that the designer unisex fragrance on his dresser was extravagant. Once they arrived at the top of the sled path, they all lined up.

Jordan rode down with the girl between his legs. They took the path in the woods instead of the clear hillside. The trees and bushes with their bald limbs whizzed by as they slid down the compacted snow. Halfway down the slope, the sled stopped. The girl turned around and, quicker than a rabbit running from a dog, a tongue was inserted into her mouth. A wet, sloppy, jousting experience that was over quickly, thank goodness. She was taken aback, but she had nowhere to go. Was this supposed to be better than just kissing on the lips? She wasn't convinced at this point. She also couldn't help but feel that it was an orchestrated attempt to assemble the necessary precursors to getting that home run.

This girl was very intuitive, and she had felt for some time that Jordan wasn't being truthful with her. They didn't talk about anything but music. There was no real spark except her addiction to his smell and his almost mohawk. She decided it would be best to break up with him over the phone on Monday after school.

After the deed was done, Dave came over for a huddle. He told her that she should have just slept with him. The girl wasn't sure whether he understood that SHE had broken up with HIM. And then he relayed some news. Jordan had another girlfriend in Southbury. They didn't break up when he moved to Milford.

The girl wasn't very familiar with the notion of cheating, but she immediately felt a hollowness arise in her chest. The glassy sparkle that inhabited her eyes faded a bit. She knew that everything would be OK. She knew she hadn't done anything wrong. And she was grateful that she exited when she did. If Jordan wanted to be fast and furious, then he could do it with his original lady. And as for Dave keeping this secret, she now understood why he urged her to submit. He knew that she didn't stand a chance if she wasn't going to keep up. Thankfully, Jordan soon moved back to Southbury.

The girl rated her first real French kissing experience low. She wondered which variables would contribute to a different, more enjoyable experience. She hoped that it would be less wet next time. Moisture freezes fast in winter. She didn't want to walk around with an icicle face.

Oh my new year

because I am a year
older now,
I have to pull my
laptop closer
to my face in
order to read
your poems.

our dance

lateral movement

sweater greens
and heather


continuum

uprising

# You touched me

You touched my hair while I was in the shower. You cupped my head from behind with your big hand, just slightly. Just enough to let me know you were there. I don't think you realized where I was at the time. You're not the kind of person to intrude like that. You must be at your computer, yes. That's what I saw when I asked you what you were doing. Writing about me, I suppose. Although flattered, like always, I wonder why we are starting this again. What is the purpose of this? Does it really further any cause or add any greatness to our endeavors? I think we are just postponing our own lives. Another way to procrastinate. "Can I at least see it?" I asked. You said yes. So where is it?

But then I realized that it wasn't you. Someone is impersonating you in the fog. Tricky of whoever it is...they must have been spying on me for some time now. I knew it when it sat on the bed. You would never do that. I thought that I would be disappointed when it sank in that you weren't around. I really didn't mind the intrusion. I am relieved, though. We are done with the foolery. And now on to the real things.

funksucksink

In bed under rainbow
Afghan
autumn leaves wind
don't throw
your dead at me.
turn around

# Reaching

I'm
without even
a game. Cut

off.
my own
doing. Now what?

picking up the comments

you've become a real woman
thanks
your hair is long
it's dead
it looks nice like that
did my hair look bad?
your hair's gotten long
it changed your face shape
what does that mean?
nice pants
yeah, check out my ass in these!
i look forward to seeing what you're going to wear now
ok
you have cute stuff
now i wear it
you don't have to work
i still work
i hate you
that's a compliment coming from you
where's little mousy?
heh...
wow, your hair's gotten long
uhh
cute shoes
i like shoes
with animals it's defensiveness
yeah, i didn't feel anything

always wondered

what would I
be without
rules?

Many Suns

laughter wish, yearn to speak. languid
plants. molded with
silence.

sunlit wake. the new way.
love that blue.

bother not clouds. drink me from
the sky. learn your tongue and let
me rest from shining.

unknown past. seedling

no hope but to rise, meet it's
master.

some day.

# Equilibrium

I am not fazed by death.
To live equally in both worlds
bears a resemblance to insanity;
for not a care can touch the soul
and not one angel's voice goes unheard.

Sick Belly

The cake tasted,
what's the
word?

Tangy.
But I
ate it anyway.

storm

in the lightning
in the electric rain
new nests flow downstream

Indeed, thank you

For the twirling
nervous belly
dance.

2:07 am

I don't know where to go.
I am sweaty and tired.
I just received an automated email response.

Too Many Words

Hard cock nights
of boogie woogie
dreams transition
star-wise into my
immediate need for you.

Peace Meal

So into you
care about
me.

## Confused Clouds

Bicycle mailman, trashcan blue
Camry. Imitations of my
clouds blocking sky. I went
to the shore, from across
the bridge to find sponge.

This is my sky. Structure
roof, array of colors. Poke
through air, backdrop, not
solid. Empty garage we
dwell with cats, plastic
tubs, and weeds so beautiful
grow through the floor.

White top seeds spreading
generations. We can knock
down this structure and
not lose a thing.

First Kiss 3: Interlude

He sat on the floor of her 10x10-foot bedroom. The wood-grained linoleum that made painting practical but sitting rough didn't even faze him. His legs crossed, and knees elevated. His blue eyes large and eager to see what she was about to do to him. She mesmerized him. The wild tendrils of his hair similar to his frenetic energy. He wished to touch her always. The way she would always place her ankle next to his when they slept. She finally sat on the cold floor and faced him. Told him to close his eyes. Placed her hands on his shoulders lightly. She entered him in spirit. Her extended being swam in his body, searching for dark spots, for hidden poetry, for places that would make him giggle. All with her mind, she'd give and get sensations. To him, it was real. To her, it was natural. And as this rummage was taking place, they kissed. A metaphor for her deeper pursuit, a way to be invited in. To let his guard down. To feel safe.

Before I Draw

I like to call them chalk
because when they are
inviting me so subtly
to pick them up, the
slightest matter surrounding
them blows to the sides
and not a pastel could
pull off the vibrancy
they represent themselves as.

## Bitsy Chaos

The stars are
only puzzle
pieces

tossed up in
frustration. When
they

fall,
I make
my planner full.

Equinox

A season between.
Now that's
freedom.

spinal tap at work not involving needles but
sitting backside to a large box.


It wasn't my work.
There was a staff meeting called after hours, it was a cafe
or a futuristic pizza place, where everyone
was sitting on tables and waiting their turns for the spinal
tap machine.
I sat next to a blond man on the table, waiting for my
friend, and we held hands.
He then melted into a belt buckle and attached to my
pants so I walked him around the table a few times.
We sat back on the table, he unmelted, thanked me for
the walk, reached into his pocket, and gave me his card.

Sleeping days

an emergence of
will
to rectify

a life
lived on the
floor

# Pro Se

There is usually something better
than what you are experiencing
at the moment.

If you can't imagine it
then you are screwed.

I have no advice for
attaining the better,
but always keep in mind
that life can be cruel

Until the point of
surrender.

Past them

I wear: three shirts with
differing sleeve lengths,
two varieties of undergarments,
a pair of unmatched fuzzy socks,
gray serger-seamed pants with wet cuffs,
an orange elastic,
green and black glasses.
Underneath is: skin, hair, nails, eyes, teeth, tongue, ears,
lips.
Soft, dizzy, and cold.
Beyond this innermost nothing:
I see my eyes and look deeply
past the green of them,
while speaking, I seem comedic,
what's left is a frozen moment of silence.

# Break-up

Wait!  We never
used the
handcuffs...

Grumpy

Even this latte
tastes like
wood.

# Hot Damn

Yes, I am a superhero Goddess.
But there is a reason my wings
are hidden from view: it's so
you don't see me coming.

Bikini Day #1

There is something
so satisfying
about

finding
sand in
my belly button.

## Listening to Cherbourg

Ain't nothing pretty
enough for this day
that I could say,

so I'm soakin' deep
the sunshine like a
freshly unfurled leaf.

And when I do

If there is something
deep in the valley,
for instance, a shallow
dug out place in a
low-lying stream, one
left by a child who
overturned a rock,
then I'll find it.

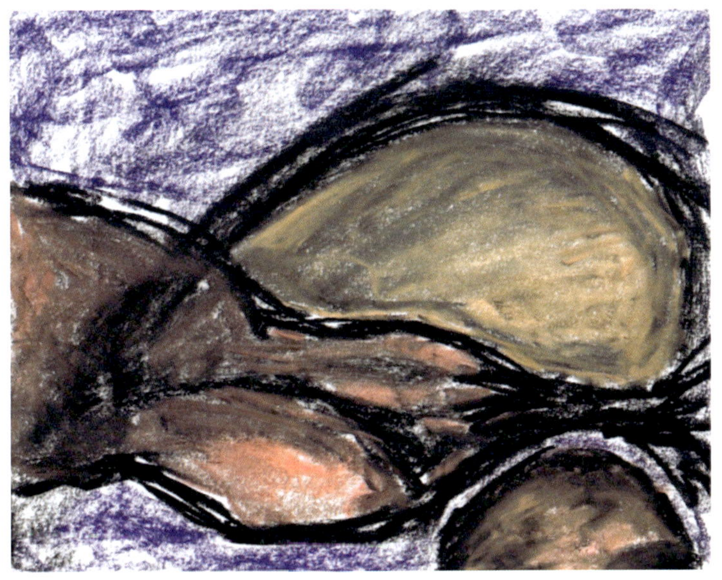

Residue

Wash yourself. You
smell like
me.

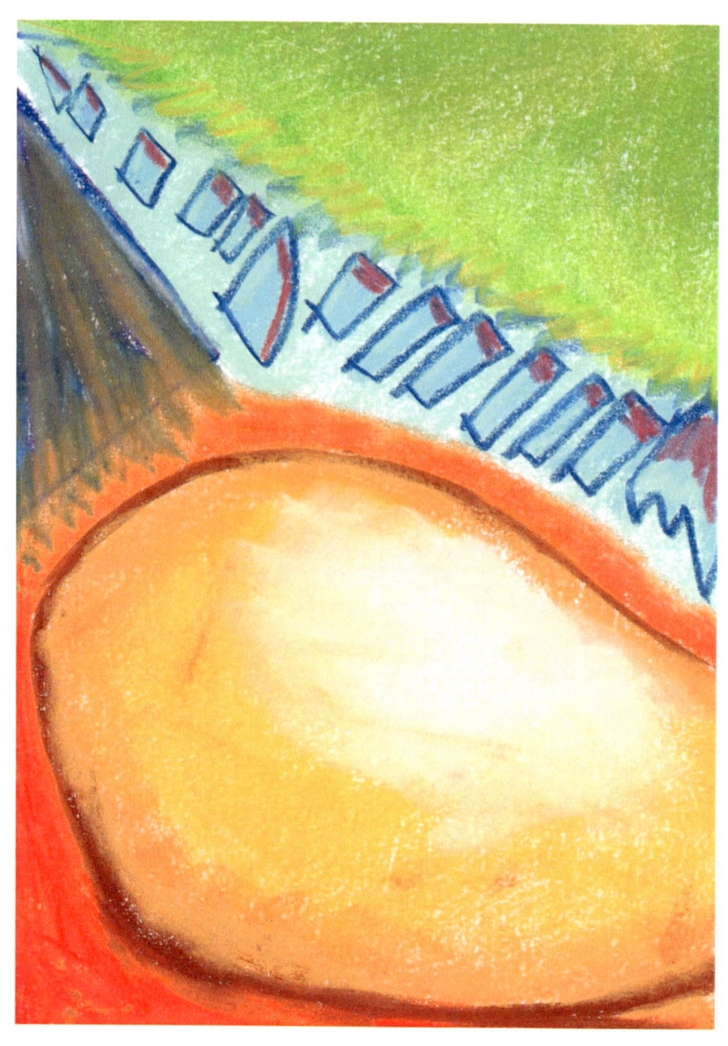

# First Kiss 4: Couches

Tiger blanket on a twin bed, an undressed brown pillow that rarely got used, no headboard, a big desk, and dead candles everywhere. This is the bedroom of a teenage girl desperately trying to meet Billy Corgan, who feels sexy in oversized corduroy work pants.

She noticed this one day in a parking lot, walking from the car to the mall entrance with her mother and sister. The sand colored pants hung low on one hip, with her father's ancient t-shirt faded to a pale yellow on top. The stretch of skin exposed by the falling pants and hiked-up cotton hemline of her shirt sent a bite of recognition of what it feels like to be sensual into her brain.

Skater, grunge, whatever you'd call her look didn't matter. Her friend was a real skater, and only the shoes mattered. They had to grip a board and manipulate the rectangle into flipping and landing safely. She could never figure out the geometry of such feats. She preferred inline skates, something that would later be referred to as "fruitbooting." Aggressive inline skaters never garnered much respect from the community, but she was a girl, which meant everything.

Paul was over 6 feet tall, had dirty blonde hair down to his nipples, and looked exactly like the lead singer of Silverchair. The band was very popular at the time, and any mention of it near Paul would make him squirm with disgust. She first saw him from the car as her mother pulled up to High School orientation. She spotted him on the sidewalk talking to another kid and knew instantly that they would be friends.

He was extremely kind-hearted and the most honest person she'd ever met, but he lacked a sense of decorum about race and religion that I don't think he ever reconciled. One year for her birthday, Paul made the girl a mobile. She was very crafty herself and was touched by the time and skill he put into this present. It was constructed of rope, large washers and metal fittings, the hard-plastic head of a toy Kermit the Frog doll, and at the top was a swastika drawn onto a piece of cardboard. The girl and her Mother's family are Jewish. He knew this. To her 17-year-old mind, he didn't mean harm. he was just that kind of guy.

The girl always thought that Paul was from Tree Fort, Louisiana, because she couldn't decipher Shreveport when he said it. A mutual friend from school told the girl that Paul was color blind. Once she confirmed this by administering the green-light/red-light test, she started having some fun. Corey, the same kid Paul had been talking to on orientation day, would give Paul pink and purple lighters and tell him they were red or blue. They would convince Paul that the girl's hair was orange when it was really green. They would try and tease him at least once a day to make him feel desired and part of the inner circle. Paul was also the girl's lab partner in Biology. She would make him do all of the gross stuff, like the cheek swab and the insect-related investigations.

Eventually, the girl made enough friends at her new school to get invited to parties. Paul had no problem showing up at places where he didn't know anyone. So he was certainly happy to go with the girl to wherever the fun would be. I wouldn't say she discovered beer at these parties, but she did discover the compulsion this bubbly beverage caused.

One particularly warm night, the girl descended into the basement of Melanie's house and found Paul standing by the open garage door. He was smoking a cigarette, something the girl wouldn't start doing for another year. She approached him with a big swivel in her hips. It was not a forced or conscious movement. Her chin felt strange, and her ears were alert, and as soon as she noticed these physiological abnormalities, she was at Paul's side, taking in the scent of his Parliament. She turned her fizzy head toward his and grabbed his flannel with her small fist and tugged. His reaction was, "Whhhaaatt?" with a long, dramatic sense of dismay.

She tugged again, but this time pulling in a downward motion. "Come here!" she said sternly while cracking a smile. He flicked his cigarette butt onto the sloped driveway and exhaled before turning his head back in her direction. He bent forward, enough to reach his mouth to hers, and gave her one last look of intention. As if to ask if this is what she wanted. She again smiled and connected their mouths before he had the chance to back away.

The stance was all wrong, but all they cared about was the feeling of joy their tongues produced in the regions of their bodies that mattered. They moved each other about with their hands, finding angles and pockets, and soft spots that enhanced their encounter. They felt so natural at this. This felt right, and would even without the beer.

This was their friendship now. They made out in front of people, dogs, and cats. They got caught by her father at least a dozen times. The scene would be: Dad's head popping past the door frame, the girl notices and quickly pulls away from Paul while swiping her arm across her mouth to dry it off. Everyone laughing. (Dad took this in stride; he liked Paul.)

At one important New Year's party at Melanie's house, Paul was late. The girl had been drinking and felt her chin get heavy, and her body start to feel needy. This waiting enhanced her symptoms but made them irritating. When Paul finally arrived, she approached him with speed. She whispered, "Standing isn't going to cut it this time. Let's lie down."

Paul's reaction showed a conflict. She couldn't decipher what his exact thoughts were, but he walked away, which made the girl even more irked. Later that evening, he found her, and she got her wish. It was still very much friendly, clothed, and extremely satisfying. What colored her world was this ability to get what she wanted. She never asked for too much, but she never let others' views stain her picture.

There were many drunken make-outs to come. More couches, more lying down, more dads. Later on in life, more sex. More bumbling nights of staying over and staying just friends. One night, the girl sat on the edge of his very comfortable Bob's Discount Furniture mattress and looked down. She started feeling full of emotion. They had been drinking, but more than that, they were sitting next to each other on a bed the same way they had 14 years ago. "Paul, I want to tell you something serious, and I mean it in a really sincere way. I love you. You mean so much to me."

Once again, there was a hesitation from him. She assured him that it was still just as a friend that she loved him. She knew that he'd always wanted a bit more. It was easier to ignore this fact, though, and it was something he was willing to do as well. Love, to the girl, is an open thing. It cannot be limited to one being or shaded into one expression. He did reciprocate her kind words. She could feel their truth as they wrapped around her in the dark.

9. 6.08

Soak you up
I could,
yeah

Sunk

I'd rather sink down deep
than
show you my dinosaur scales

I don't want to go to sleep yet

It could have been a hat, but it looked like green hair.
Listened to some good advice over and over and over.
Made some funny noises while dancing to the stove.
Grapefruit body wash put aside for the mud soap.
Cleaned the chalk dust from the kitchen table.
Drank some arnica flower essence in water.
Turned myself on once buying a bra.
My collarbone really freaks me out.
I was definitely a man before.
Grey's anatomy is on tv.
Not tired, yet.
Wet hair.
Shhh.

Desperate

I'd eat my
chalk for
you

Today

On checkerboard linoleum
in the
dark

lodge,
peeking through
the evergreen's needles.

Alien

I
feel sexy
in oversized work

pants, purple lipstick,
and butterfly
eyes.

www.ingramcontent.com/pod-product-compliance
Lightning Source LLC
Chambersburg PA
CBRC090712070726
47599CB00032B/1038